THAT'S
A
GOOD
QUESTION!

WILLIAM
MacDONALD

ECS
MINISTRIES
The Word to the World

That's a Good Question!

William MacDonald

Published by:
ECS Ministries
PO Box 1028
Dubuque, IA 52004-1028
phone: (563) 585-2070
email: ecsorders@ecsministries.org
website: www.ecsministries.org

First ECS Edition 2014

ISBN 978-1-59387-218-2

Code: W-TAGQ

Copyright © 1995, 2014 William MacDonald

Previously published by Walterick Publishers.

Printed in the United States of America

You've Got Questions. God Is the Answer!

Contents

INTRODUCTION

NOTHING HAPPENS IN life by chance. Everything is planned or permitted.

It was no chance that this booklet came into your hands.

It contains truths which, if accepted, could change the whole direction of your life. Not only that—it describes how you can enjoy forgiveness of sins, peace with God, and the assurance of a home in heaven after this life is over.

The following pages answer questions that you may have been thinking. Certainly it answers questions that everyone should be asking.

Take a few minutes to read it carefully.

The last answer is the crucial one. If you take the action suggested, you will be forever grateful.

Guarantee

THE BIBLE CARRIES a guarantee with it. You'll find it in John 7:17. It's a promise from God that anyone who sincerely wants to know the truth will find it.

Put it to the test. Ask God to reveal Himself to you. Then as you read this booklet, pay particular attention to the Bible verses that are quoted.

The next few minutes could be the most important ones in your life. If you respond to God's message as found in His Word, you will be the possessor of eternal life.

THAT'S A GOOD QUESTION!

What is the most important thing in life?

It's important to have health, but it's not of maximum importance, because some time in the normal course of events we will all have to die.

It's important to have money and possessions, but they are not enough. Some day we will have to leave them all behind.

It's important to have pleasure, but even that doesn't last forever.

In view of the shortness of time and the length of eternity, the most important thing is to know that our eternal destiny is safely assured. It is to know that our afterlife will be spelled H-E-A-V-E-N and not H-E-L-L.

Jesus asked this crucial question: "What will it profit a man if he gains the whole world, and loses his own soul? Or what will a man give in exchange for his soul" (Mark 8:36-37).

Why is there any problem?
Why is there any question about it?

The problem is sin. Sin has separated man from God, has made him unfit for heaven, and has richly qualified him for hell.

The Bible says, "Your iniquities have separated you from your God, and your sins have hidden His face from you" (Isa. 59:2).

What is sin?

Sin is anything short of God's perfection. That is what God means when He says that "all have sinned and fall short of the glory of God" (Rom. 3:23).

It is doing what we know we should not do. "All unrighteousness is sin" (1 John 5:17).

It is failing to do what we know we should do. "To him who knows to do good and does not do it, to him it is sin" (James 4:17).

It is violating the conscience. "Whatever is not from faith is sin" (Rom. 14:23).

It is self-will or lawlessness. It's saying to God, "Not Your will but mine be done."

Not only are our thoughts, words, and deeds sinful, but our inner lives are sinful. In fact, what we are is a lot worse than anything we have ever done.

You make me feel guilty. Don't you
want me to have a good self image?

God wants you to feel guilty so you will be moved to take action. Only those who admit they are sick will go to a doctor for healing.

Didn't the Lord Jesus say, "Those who are well have no need of a physician but those who are sick" (Luke 5:31)? Only those who acknowledge that they are sinners will go to Christ for salvation. What's the use of having a good self image when you are sliding over the edge of a precipice?

If good people go to heaven and bad people go to hell, then what do I have to worry about?

The premise is wrong and therefore the conclusion is wrong.

The premise is wrong. It is not true that good people go to heaven. According to God's standard, there are no good people. "For there is not a just man on earth who does good and does not sin" (Eccl. 7:20).

The only kind of people who go to heaven are sinners saved by grace.

Because the premise is wrong, the conclusion is wrong. If you are not saved by grace, you have plenty to worry about.

Do you mean to say I'm as bad as a lot of other people I know?

From your own standpoint, or from the standpoint of your relatives and that count. The Bible says that those who measure themselves by themselves and compare themselves among themselves are not wise (see 2 Cor. 10:12). It is God's standpoint that counts. In God's sight we are guilty sinners.

If I keep the Ten Commandments and do the best I can, isn't that enough?

First of all, you should realize what the Ten Commandments require:

1. No other gods. The true God must have first place. This eliminates the mythical gods of the heathen but also such gods as money, sex, power, self. None of these can be on the throne of the life.

2. No idol. We usually think of idols as graven images. but this commandment also forbids worshiping such things as a car, house, wife, or children.

3. Don't take the Name of the Lord in vain. This forbids testifying falsely when under oath but also rules out profanity and cursing.

4. Remember the Sabbath Day. We should set one day in seven apart for the worship and service of God.

5. Honor your father and mother. Don't disobey them, treat them disrespectfully, or steal from them. It also involves caring for them and showing gratitude to them.

6. Don't kill. Even if you have never actually killed someone, remember that we are all guilty of the murder of the Son of God. It was our sins that caused His death. Jesus taught that hatred and anger are murder in embryo (Matt. 5:21-22; 1 John 3:15). Certainly abortion is a current form of murder.

7. Don't commit adultery. This forbids all sex outside of marriage. But Jesus also taught that even the lustful look is adulterous (Matt. 5:28).

8. Don't steal. Don't take your neighbor's property but also don't rob God of service, worship, obedience, and glory.

9. Don't lie. Don't file false income tax returns. Don't lie about your age. Don't tell white lies or fibs. Don't exaggerate or deceive.

10. Don't covet. Coveting takes place in the mind, so this means "Have a pure thought life." How is your thought life?

Jesus summarized the commandments by saying that we should love God with all our being and love our neighbor as our self.

No one, apart from the Lord Jesus, has ever kept them, or can keep them.

If we can't keep the Ten Commandments, why were they given?

They were given to convict us of the fact that we are sinners. "By the law is the knowledge of sin" (Rom. 3:20). It takes a straight line to reveal a crooked one. The commandments are God's straight line. We stand next to them and realize how crooked we are.

But they were never intended as a stepladder to heaven. A mirror tells us our face needs washing, but the mirror doesn't clean it. A thermometer tells us we have a fever, but swallowing a thermometer doesn't cure a fever.

Isn't there any way I can atone or make up for my own sins?

There is no way.

Do you mean to say that I have been wrong in doing penance for my sins?

The word "penance" is not found in the Bible, neither is the idea found there.

The Bible tells us that all our righteousnesses (that is, all the best we have to offer) are no better than filthy rags (see Isa. 64:6).

It is not penance that God wants, nor mere penitence, that is, sorrow for sin, nor remorse, but repentance.

What do you mean by repentance?

Repentance is a change of mind about sin, self, God, and Christ, which changes the attitude, which changes the actions. It involves not just the mind but the conscience. It is the sinner's acknowledgment of his ungodliness, lostness, helplessness, and hopelessness, and his need of grace. It is an about face. It is taking sides with God against one's self.

It involves penitence, that is, sorrow for sin, but it is more than this. You can be sorry for sin and yet not turn away from it.

Isn't there some way I can earn or merit my salvation? That would please me very much.

That is why salvation by works is such a popular teaching. It is popular because it makes men think that they can be their own savior. It gives a place of honor to man's sinful nature.

But there is no way you can earn or deserve salvation. God says that we are saved by grace alone (Eph. 2:8-9).

You keep saying that salvation is by grace. What do you mean by that?

Grace is God showing favor to those who don't deserve it, but who, in fact, deserve the very opposite.

It is closely linked with the idea of a gift. You do not earn a gift. That would be wages. You receive a gift and say "thank you."

Grace and works cannot be mixed. It has to be one or the other.

Grace must be distinguished from justice. In justice, you get what you deserve. In grace you get favor that you don't deserve.

Then do I understand that you don't believe in good works?

As we have already noted, God's word teaches that we are not saved by good works, but once we are saved, we should be characterized by good works. Good works are not the cause, they are the effect; not the root but the fruit; not the origin but the result.

The first good work that anyone can do is to believe on Christ (John 6:29). From then on anything he does for the glory of God and for the good of others is a good work.

I was baptized when I was a baby. Isn't that enough?

Baptism saves no one, neither babies nor adults.

There is not a single verse in the New Testament to support the baptism of babies. The only people who were baptized were those who had trusted Jesus Christ as Lord and Savior (Acts 2:41).

The teaching that baptism saves babies makes God an unjust Judge, condemning those who never had the chance to be baptized.

It makes water the Savior instead of Jesus.

If infants could be saved by a few drops of water, then why did the Lord Jesus have to die?

It simply doesn't work. Many who were baptized as infants have turned out to be adulterers, murderers, and other types of criminals.

Look! Put it to me simply. What do I need in order to be saved?

You need to be born again. Jesus said it tersely, "Do not marvel that I said to you, 'You must be born again'" (John 3:7). Unless a person is born again, he will never see or enter the kingdom of God.

What do you mean by being born again?

The new birth is a marvelous, miraculous, supernatural work of God that takes place when a person repents of his sins and receives Jesus Christ by faith as Lord and Savior. Your first birth was physical; the new birth is spiritual.

You say that the only way to be saved is through faith in Christ. Isn't it narrow minded to think that there is only one way?

Then the Bible is narrow minded.

Jesus said that no one could come to God, the Father, except through Him (John 14:6).

Peter said that no one could be saved in any other way than through Christ (Acts 4:12).

And Paul wrote that there is no other foundation except Jesus Christ (1 Cor. 3:11).

Faith in Christ is the only way of salvation.

What does it mean to have faith or to believe?

It means to accept the Lord Jesus Christ alone as your only hope for heaven. You renounce any idea of saving yourself or even having part in your own salvation and you place your full confidence in Him.

Various synonyms for believing are used in the Bible such as:

Receive. Enter the door. Open a door. Eat. Drink. Come or come home—like the prodigal son. Accept a gift. Look. Love. Confess. Hear. Touch—the hem of His garment. Accept an invitation: to a wedding or to a great feast. Follow.

Isn't faith a leap in the dark?

No. Actually faith demands the surest evidence, and finds it in the Word of God. There is nothing as certain as God's word. His word is truth (John 17:17). To trust Him is the most sane, logical, reasonable thing a person can do. What is more reasonable than that the creature should trust his Creator? He cannot lie, deceive, or be deceived.

Isn't the gospel too easy? Too cheap?

It is easy to be saved—so easy that it is available to all.

It is cheap for the sinner—without money and without price (Isa. 55:1).

However, it wasn't cheap for the Savior. He had to leave Heaven's glory, come down to this jungle of sin, suffer, shed His precious blood, die a horrible death in order to purchase our pardon (1 Peter 2:24).

How can I tell if I have believed in the right way, if I have enough faith, or if I have the right kind of faith?

Faith is not the savior. Jesus is. True faith lays hold of Him.

It's not intellectual assent to facts but trust in a Person.

It's not the amount of faith but the Object of faith that matters.

You say that you don't have to do anything to be saved, that all you have to do is believe. Isn't that a contradiction?

It sounds like a contradiction but here is what is meant.

There is nothing meritorious that you have to do (or can do). You are not saved by good works, church membership, faithfulness in obeying the sacraments, giving to the poor, etc (Titus 3:5).

Believing on Christ is not a meritorious work. You don't earn heaven by doing it, nor can you boast because you did it.

How can I know that I'll be able to hold out after I'm saved?

You will be no more able to keep yourself saved than you were to save yourself in the first place.

Christ not only saves but also keeps. When He begins a good work in you, He will finish it (Phil. 1:6; Jude 24).

If all you have to do is believe, then can't you go out and live any way you want?

When you are saved, God changes your wants. You no longer want to sin. You lose your fierce appetite for sin. You don't want to go on in that which caused the death of your Savior. You have a love of holiness. The Bible says, "Therefore, if anyone is in Christ, he is a new creation; old things have passed away; behold, all things have become new" (2 Cor. 5:17).

If I sin after I'm saved, don't I lose my salvation?

Jesus said that no sheep of His will ever perish (John 10:27-29).

All who are justified will one day be glorified (Rom. 8:30b).

Salvation is a birth (John 3:3, 5). A birth is final and unchangeable.

Salvation means eternal life (John 3:16, 36). Eternal is forever.

Nothing can separate the believer from the love of God (Rom. 8:38-39).

But I know a man who was saved, then he sinned and was lost. What do you have to say to that?

If he was genuinely saved, he couldn't be lost. If, however, he was only a false professor, then he could have experienced a sort of moral reformation. He may have turned over a new leaf, and then lapsed back into his old, sinful ways.

We must not base our doctrine on experience but only on the inspired Word of God. The test must always be, "What does the Bible say?"

You say that when a person is saved, he receives forgiveness of sins. But what about sins committed after he is saved?

When a person is saved, he receives forgiveness for all his sins as far as the penalty is concerned. When Jesus died, He died for all our sins, past, present, and future. At the time He died, they were all future. He died for them all. Now God, the Judge, cannot find any sins on the believer for which to punish him with eternal death because Jesus bore the punishment on the cross of Calvary. "There is therefore now no condemnation to those who are in Christ Jesus" (Rom. 8:1).

Sins committed after salvation have several results:

➢ They break fellowship with God. This fellowship remains broken until the sin is confessed and forsaken. However, although fellowship is broken, relationship is not. Fellowship is a tender thread; relationship is an unbreakable chain.

➢ They break fellowship with our fellow believers.

➢ They hinder our prayers from being answered.

➢ They make service for Christ unfruitful, if not impossible. They seal our lips.

➢ They bring dishonor and reproach on the Name of the Lord.

➢ They rob us of joy.

➢ They cast doubt on the reality of our conversion. J. I. Packer said, "The only proof of past conversion is present convertedness."

➢ They hinder spiritual growth.

➢ They invite God's discipline.

The unbeliever receives judicial forgiveness of sins by believing on the Lord Jesus Christ. It is a once-for-all forgiveness.

The believer receives parental forgiveness by confession. It is something we need as long as we are in the body.

What happens if, after I'm saved, I die with unconfessed sins?

As explained above, the penalty of those sins has already been paid. God will not demand payment twice. So your eternal salvation is unaffected.

The fellowship that was broken by sins will be restored when you pass into the presence of the Lord. Unconfessed sins may result in a loss of reward at the Judgment Seat of Christ.

You say that Christ died for all. Why then aren't all saved?

The death of Christ was sufficient for all the sins of all people of all times. But it is only effective when a person receives Christ by faith.

God doesn't save people against their will. He isn't going to populate heaven with people who don't want to be there.

If I trust Christ, will I have a great emotional experience?

Some do and some don't. To some, especially those saved from lives of deep sin, there is often a dramatic experience of deliverance. To others it may be the quiet acceptance of a divine offer. There is no question that salvation involves the emotions, but sometimes the emotional impact may not come until later, and even then, over a period of time.

How will I know it when I am saved?

First and foremost through the Word of God. The Bible was written so that those who believe on the Name of the Son of God may know that they are saved (1 John 5:13).

But there are also these evidences:

➢ A desire to obey the Lord.
➢ A love for Christians.
➢ A love of holiness.

➢ A hatred of sin.

➢ A love for the Word of God.

➢ A love of prayer.

➢ A consciousness of God's guidance.

➢ A steadfast continuance in the faith.

➢ The witness of the indwelling Holy Spirit.

➢ A desire to share the good news with others.

Don't I have to clean up my act before I come to Jesus?

That is not the gospel. The more you try, the worse you will get.

What you need is not reformation but regeneration.

The dying thief couldn't clean up his act and neither can you.

Jesus told about a man who tried to clean up his act. His house was cleaned and empty but he didn't let the Savior in. His latter end was worse than his first (Matt. 12:43-45).

> Let not conscience make you linger,
> Nor of fitness fondly dream;
> All the fitness He requires
> Is to feel your need of Him.
>
> Come, you weary, heavy-laden,
> Lost and ruined by the fall
> If you tarry till you're better,
> You will never come at all.

Isn't it presumption for a person to say that he is saved?

If his salvation depended in any way on his own righteousness, then it would be presumption. But when a true believer says he is saved, he is not boasting. He is saying in effect, "I did all the sinning and Christ did all the saving." He attributes his salvation to the grace of God and not to himself.

The greatest presumption is to call God a liar by not believing the testimony that He has given concerning His Son (1 John 5:10).

If you Christians are right, why are there so few of you?

The question assumes that the majority is usually or always right. This is not true.

In the time of the flood, only eight people were right; the rest all perished. At Calvary, the crowd was wrong; only a handful of fearful disciples were right.

Jesus said, "Wide is the gate and broad is the way that leads to destruction, and there are many who go in by it. Because narrow is the gate and difficult is the way which leads to life, and there are few that find it" (Matt. 7:13-14).

If God is all-powerful, why does He allow wars, tragedies, suffering, and sorrow?

All these things are the result of sin having entered the world. God is not the originator of any evil. All sickness, suffering, sorrow, and death come from the devil. God permits it, but then overrules it for His glory, for the good of His people, and for the outworking of His purposes.

If God is a God of love, how could He send people to hell?

First of all, God did not make hell for people. He made it for the devil and His angels. God does not want any human being to go to hell. In order to prevent it, He sent His Son to suffer, bleed and die on Calvary to provide a way of escape. If people refuse God's way of salvation, what alternative is there? In a real sense, the only people who go to hell are those who choose to—those who deliberately reject the free gift of everlasting life in heaven.

What bothers me is that there are so many hypocrites in the church.

It is important to remember that there is a difference between real Christians and nominal Christians, between those who only say they are Christians and those who show by their lives that they are true believers. There are hypocrites in politics but that doesn't stop people from voting. There are hypocrites in athletics but people still swarm to watch them. There are hypocrites in the entertainment world but that doesn't turn people off. There is counterfeit money but that doesn't cause anyone to refuse to have money. Men only counterfeit what is real and valuable. We do not try to excuse hypocrisy, but don't use it as an excuse for not being saved. God does not ask you to believe in Christians; He asks you to believe in Jesus. When you become a Christian, be sure that you show the world what a genuine Christian should be.

I hesitate because I believe that all the church wants is my money.

Sometimes this is used as an excuse for not becoming a Christian. It is not a valid one. While it is true that certain churches, radio, and

TV programs have become money-making rackets, that is not an accurate representation of the true Christian faith. God doesn't want your money; He wants your full, confiding trust.

If I get saved, do I have to be baptized?

If you are truly converted, you should want to be baptized. Although it is not necessary for salvation, it is necessary for obedience. Because Jesus commanded it, it is very important (Matt. 28:19). It is one of the first ways you can make a confession of your faith to the world. If a person stubbornly refuses to be baptized, this refusal casts doubt on the reality of his conversion experience. Professing Christians who die unbaptized will be unbaptized for all eternity.

If that faith denies the deity of Christ, or if it teaches salvation by works, or if it practices idolatry, or if it denies that the Bible is the Word of God, yes, you will have to leave it. You will want to leave it, even if it causes conflict in your family.

Jesus said, "Do not think that I came to bring peace on earth. I did not come to bring peace but a sword. For I have come to set a man against his father, a daughter against her mother, and a daughter-in-law against her mother-in-law; and a man's enemies will be those of his own household" (Matt. 10:34-36). Conversion often alienates relatives against the new believer.

However, that should not discourage you. Experience proves that when a new convert lives a consistent life before his family, they are eventually led to the Lord or at least become less hostile and more accepting.

The believer's responsibility is to obey the Lord and leave the consequences to Him. He always rewards obedience.

I feel that I should trust Christ, and yet I am afraid to do it. Can you tell me what is the trouble?

It could be one of several things.

It could be pride.

It could be that you are ashamed of Jesus. It could be that you want your sins rather than Christ, that you want pleasure more than holiness.

It could be your love for some person who is an unbeliever.

It could be family pressure-fear of the reaction of your parents.

I'm afraid I will have to give up too much if I become a Christian. The cost is too high.

Have you ever considered the cost of not becoming a Christian?

I think I'll put it off until later in life. Isn't that OK?

You have forgotten two things. One is the uncertainty of life. The other is the possibility of the any-moment coming of the Lord.

I admit that I could be killed suddenly in an accident, but what's that about the Lord's coming?

Jesus promised His followers that He would come again. No one knows the time; it could be today. There are many indications that it might be soon. At that time true believers will be caught away to heaven. Unbelievers who have heard the gospel and rejected it will have no more chance to be saved. They will pass into a time of terrible tribulation on earth and eventually into hell itself.

Are you talking about the end of the world?

No, there are several things that will happen before the end of the world. First, as already mentioned, Jesus will come and take the church home to heaven. Then after a period of intense trouble on earth He will return to set up His kingdom. That kingdom will last for 1,000 years. At the end of the time, the world as we now know it will come to an end. It will be dissolved by fire. That will usher in the eternal state in which there will be new atmospheric and stellar heavens and a new earth.

Ok, then, tell me once more, as simply as you can, how I can be saved and sure of it.

First, you must acknowledge before God that you are a guilty, lost sinner and that you deserve the punishment of eternal death.

Also, you must abandon any idea of saving yourself or even contributing to your salvation by good character or good works of any kind.

Next, you must believe that the Lord Jesus Christ died as a Substitute for you, paying the penalty that your sins deserved.

Finally, by a definite act of faith, you must receive Him as your exclusive Lord and Savior, your only hope for heaven.

When you do this in utter sincerity, you can know on the authority of God's word that you are saved for time and for eternity.

Here is God's promise: "For God so loved the world that He gave His only begotten Son, that whoever believes in Him should not perish but have everlasting life" (John 3:16).

You have everything to gain and nothing to lose.

Will you believe? Right now?

At a fashionable gathering of prominent people, a young lady played and sang with such finesse and beauty that the audience rocked the hall with applause.

Afterwards a Christian named Caesar Malan thanked her for her singing. But then in extended conversation, he gracefully made a transition to her spiritual condition. She was indignant that he would even suggest that she was a sinner and that she needed to be saved. She did not respond well to the promise that the blood of Jesus Christ, God's Son, could cleanse her from all sin. After a curt rebuke, she walked away from him.

That night she could not sleep. Malan's words echoed in her mind. At 2 am she jumped out of bed, took a pencil and paper, and with tears streaming down her face, Charlotte Elliott wrote the well-known hymn, *Just As I Am*. It tells the story of how she came to Christ.

Just As I Am

Just as I am, without one plea,
But that Thy blood was shed for me
And that Thou bidd'st me come to Thee,
O Lamb of God, I come! I come!

Just as I am, and waiting not
To rid my soul of one dark blot,
To Thee whose blood can cleanse each spot,
O Lamb of God, I come! I come!

Just as I am, tho' tossed about
With many a conflict, many a doubt,
Fightings and fears within, without,
O Lamb of God, I come! I come!

Just as I am, poor, wretched, blind;
Sight, riches, healing of the mind,
Yea, all I need in Thee to find,
O Lamb of God, I come! I come!

Just as I am, Thou wilt receive,
Wilt welcome, pardon, cleanse, relieve;
Because Thy promise I believe,
O Lamb of God, I come! I come!

Just as I am, Thy love unknown
Hath broken ev'ry barrier down;
Now to be Thine, yea Thine alone,
O Lamb of God, I come! I come!

–Charlotte Elliott